Drifting in Awe

poems by

Larry D. Thacker

Finishing Line Press
Georgetown, Kentucky

Drifting in Awe

For My Wife,
My Muse,
Forever,
Karin

ACKNOWLEDGMENTS

Blood & Kudzu	*Full of Crow*, 2011
Spoken words are not our native tongue	*Full of Crow*, 2012
I can almost conjure on the weight	Mountain Heritage Literary Festival, Scarbrough Award, 3rd Place, 2012
I wonder what happened	*Country Grind*, 2014
Death of Porches	
Another birthday next week,	*Appalachian Nature Anthology*, 2016
Third week of June.	*Pikeville Review*, 2015
Cabin Echo	Mountain Heritage Literary Festival, Scarbrough Award, 1st place 2015
Home	*Appalachian Heritage*, 2013
72-degree mid-February day	*Appalachian Heritage*, 2014
Snow Blind	*O' Words Anthology*, 2015
Early April	*Five 2 One*, Sept 2016
48 hours at camp	
These growls from the forest	*Country Grind*, 2014
Medicine Bag	*Mojave River Review*, 2014
Locale Sancti	*Fried Chicken and Coffee*, 2014
Meaning	
Sing the Dead	*Southern Poetry Anthology, VI: Tennessee*, 2013
The question rises	*Moon Magazine*, 2014
When Birds Fell	*Pine Mountain Sand & Gravel*, The Dead
Crow Sun	*Still Journal*, 2012
Cold Cipher	*Still Journal*, 2015
May you know lightning	*Work To a Calm*, 2015
Nesting	
In winter, when the craziness stirs	*Kudzu Literary Magazine*, 2014
Standing Chimneys	*Broad River Review*, 2015

Publisher: Leah Maines
Editor: Christen Kincaid
Cover Art: Larry D. Thacker/painting called "Drifting in Awe"
Author Photo: Jerry Greer
Cover Design: Elizabeth Maines

Printed in the USA on acid-free paper.
Order online: www.finishinglinepress.com
also available on amazon.com

Author inquiries and mail orders:
Finishing Line Press
P. O. Box 1626
Georgetown, Kentucky 40324
U. S. A.

Table of Contents

Part I

Spoken words are not our native tongue

but rather, something deep set in the eyes,
heart-pressured pulses behind dimmed sight,

so infinitesimal and delicate to be audible
when only the swirl of amniotic fluid competed
for our attention, muffled movements just past

our shared cave of skin and muscle and heartbeat,
drifting in awe, unable to mutter what is known
before breathing. What words can relate our

transfixed view of the womb's planetarium?

I can almost conjure on the weight of the soul

It equates to something like smoke, or mists,
a smoky-charactered fog, wind enlivened,

settling calm in the body's draws and spurs,
nearly too light for gravity's notice, hiding

and exhaling, no wider than a micron, weight
of a molecule, a strung particle omicron thin,

mass of a thought, full of collapsing volume
like the most ancient of stars, heavy in their

never failing vision and memory, blood type
embedded, a mixed twist of memorial DNA,

blueprint experiences sequencing the double
helix, warmed and super coiled by God's kiss.

Wait

Wait with me a moment longer,
but watch your step over near
the porch edge. In these last
dark breaths of morning it can
be quite dangerous, indirect light

dancing pink tricks at your feet.

You might see it every day
out of the corner of your eye,
but have you hummed the sun
into being? You can sing along,
finding the lowest note you know

and drop an impossible octave.

This is the sound of the sun's
swelling over that waking ripple,
that dam of green that lightens,
blasting red-yellow into pink,
holding back what may become

the brightest scream of your life.

Ghost Branded

It's the tiniest tickle in the middle of your back,

that one aggravating spot you can never reach.

Those are your ghosts, caressing your guilt and joy,

taking their scars inventory, checking the wedding

ring tan line that won't go away, trailing the raised

outline of your healing tattoo, dabbing the sun spots

you earned last summer like fresh brown paint,

re-counting over and over the hairs of your body

and stroking tick marks in fives down your back.

Breeched

Early March and spring
is a dangerous breeched birth,

too soon and angry,
crying out from the sky womb,

destructive in sudden life
and improperly twisted,

blind and dogged for attention
and proper sacrifice.

The thawing ground turns
its eyes in fear,

hunching its back and shoulders
against the child's rolling howls,

a hunger swelling and streaking
down arms of hot light

in grasp for suckle upon
the earth's tired winter breast.

Near dark of the womb

and only a pinkish glow
lights the way, a quickened

redness of veined branches
hypnotizing, teaching my eyes

to chase the mystery of light
just past the rounded membrane's

thinness, shifts of headlights
and streetlamps, pulsed arches

timed with a heartbeat
swirling in the ears, the earliest

thoughts maybe of shorelines
or tides returning, my mother's

hummed chants and prayers,
not knowing I heard every word.

I wonder what happened

down at their own level,
in this recently lost world,
these dried packs of worms
you see on the concrete,

stilled in mid-squirm,
or twisted and sun-flat,
dry-stretched for a mysterious
thing, whatever it was gone,

a mirage perhaps, tempting
them out onto the scorched
desert concrete. Were they
worm-dancing in the rain,

called up from the ground
to some doomed gathering,
faces stretched up, smiling,
fooled by a calling promise

of bliss and wandering blind
too far from soil's safety?
Did they worry as the rains
stopped and the heat came?

Could they hear if anyone
laughed at the insanity of it all?

Fracture

The first lightning of the season visited last night,
flashes like flicked headlights against the house,
strobes in my writing room, hints of warm things
promised, but punctuated with the thunder's delay,
its faraway caution rolling and tumbling the dark.

Let this serve as reminder that good change is seldom
instant, that lightning and thunder at once behaves
as a warning that you're too close, the senses jolted
open and vulnerable. Seasons should yawn open.

No matter how cold you've become, how you despise
getting up in the morning to the bitterness of the air,
warmth will return eventually, like treating frostbite,
first with cool water, then the careful adding of heat.

You must be patient, welcoming the delayed assurance,
or the moment's brilliance will most surely take you.

Another birthday next week, same sneaking episode

as last year. A familiar creature's whistled stalk of a tune
creeping around corners, soulful invite, like greening grass
yawning to find the warmth of lathe work in the walls.

It rests in the immergence of late March song birds,
repetitive and bright. Routine. Familiar. But too much time
has passed to tell if these are the same songs as last year.
Or the same language. Or the same birds for that matter.

But it's the same message in the end, isn't it? I think so.
In the end, the same metaphor, same analogy, reliable
and eventually dreadful. Another birthday next week,
same stalking bird as last year. I am no better prepared.

Early Sunday, the last "last" cold front wanders through,
unbothered with spring's growing voice. I can't tell if it's
sprinkling rain again, or the ground is smacking its lips
competing with the dandelions. The dirt seems thirsty.

Mockingbird runs its list of languages, perched high,
practicing over a parking lot left empty by spring break,
traffic's reminder blends its hum from the highway.
A semi's rattling air brakes vibrate the ground and air.

Crows counter Robin and Starling. Bird of darkness
and snow and shiver, not giving up easily, over-watching
the arrival of concerted reminders. Crocus, come and gone,
doubling their carpet from last year, almost wholly purple.

Holy Purple. The time is near. The crow lights on a barely
greening tree, its gutterals friendly and curious, bowing
its neck and shivering. We banter, as flurries chorus up
into heavier voices, until we no longer see each other.

He calls out. I call. But the snow falls thick like wetted
powdered sugar, jetting sideways and coating everything,
clovers and onions caught off guard too fast to protest.

The crow calls a last time, gone as the sun breaks free.

Another birthday next week, same reunion with time
as before. An unfamiliar creature's hummed lullaby of a tune
curling about the corners, soulful and inviting, too much
like the yawns of Easter Lilies, or the warm willing ground.

Rare Morning

The east is flayed open
by what separates us,

pinkish flesh of the day,
just over the blue-green.

I prefer this sort of day start,
medium-rare and slow bled,

ear to the air,
sure of some hint,

some final sighs of night
straining north and south,

uncoiling sun warming
the promise of your east.

Early April

A flicking horde of bats dance down
the rumored storming firsts of spring

and willow tops in silhouette
sway like impatient giant arms,

a limbered orchestration tuned
attentive to this rogue release

of clapping thunder growling now
so anxiously beyond my view

As if awaking from a dream
the spiders whisper ever-clear

and yarn their death around the lips
of thunder heads and voiceless mists

that slink and ferry stories down
along the wind-shorn fields below

into the blessed dying town
where craters wait with missing words

The beasts will flee this place today,
pack their minds with all the bats,

and hoard their myths with all of us,

and never look back—never look back.

They say thunder is the judging voice of God,

some proof of divine jealousy through a randomized
danger. Perhaps it begins as that, but I think it morphs

to great laughter, a comedic fit barreling down through us,
rippling along all the itching places we never look,

pin-pointing the empty spots and residual warmth
of a shifting soul, God's single, never-blinking eye

studying our sprints running for the mistaken safety
of indoors, as if what doesn't see us can't hurt us.

Prey

Early spring. Three close strikes pitch down and anchor
around me, searching my grounding feet, sealing up
my animal fear, driving me from the porch. I've never
been closer to that flash of light, the exploding instant
that puffs the eyes closed and startles the heart quieter,
dredging up how close to death we all walk every day.

The monster claws its way down the road, chasing me
to the kitchen, rattling dishes and window panes,
vibrating the floor boards like mortars landing too close,
blinking the lights, birds and cicadas, squirrels frightened
to silence, hearts heavy, brittle taste of metal on my gums.

Too scared to stand still, yet afraid to move, I am reassured
of God as it crashes past in search of other needy converts.

Third week of June. Summer finally turns the corner.

Heat ripples fry from the asphalt and the smell of tar
is gentle behind the struggle of yawning Four-O-Clocks
and Day Lily perfume. It is perfectly windless here.
The smoke of two cigarettes floats in the porch eaves,
solid and lodged, nowhere to go when wind loses interest.

What is the weather there, a hundred miles south and east,
over your head? Has the wind and cool retreated to more
pleasing company, leaving me here to bake and brood?
I phone you to find out, amazed how close you can be,
though so far out of sight and in another swell of weather,
your voice back-dropped in the howls of hail and wind.

Cabin Echo

Down near the trash creek, along the path rutted out
where four wheelers blare through, etching the ground
down closer to where my peoples' steps are buried,
I try to spot where my grandfather's cabin once stood.
It is somewhere, up on that half-hidden step of land,
a flattened section, choked by webs of summer vine
framed on trees that weren't there when they were.
There, a short step off the trail, over the water
and up the steep rampart, is ground I should know,
where my family was born, where my father played.

I stumble up, wary of things low to ground that can kill me,
wondering with each lean and step where my blood stood
and walked and talked, kicking weeds back, searching south
for objects yet rotted away: chimney bricks scattered,
tin sheets rusting away, a lone concrete step, chunks of timber,
a 55-gallon drum, half a fence post, barbed wire remnants.
I puzzle it together on the spot, from stories and albums,
add my own imagined yet-born conversations, studying
what's at my feet, shifting the elements in my mind,
near my best guess where the front door might have been,
knocking at the air and wishing I knew who was home.

Porch

Front porch, late thickening of June
in fear of the rolling July, traffic out front,
housework to my back and ignored,
leaking water hose hissing judgment into a puddle,
all of it distracting me from the disturbed stacks of boxes
full of words in my head. I must frame
these disjointed belongings to sense, or die a liar.

Dog huffing at my side—bare feet
on 94-year-old porch wood, near the splinters
and dust of an old man's afternoon steps—
shadow creeps along the dog's back
and tail like a dark army of fleas.

I'm shrinking less from the dead
air's heat, that simplest part of the day's invisible
inhaling and exhaling. Look around.
All the houses here, the old ones, have porches,
folks sitting, waving, napping
and growing with their potted plants, like me.

Mosquitoes come and go, biting things.
The dog snaps in sleep, chewing
an unfinished meal, peddling legs in a fit
of galloping. The world of summer
decays faster than it can reinvent itself.

A July breeze tries lifting me from my rocker.

It suspects it can't, but I'm not so convinced.
Hints of the possibility are in the wind's practice
on less stubborn items that seldom fight back.

The neat pile of cigarette butts flinch and scatter,
my pant leg flaps and the hairs on my arms
twitch like field grass. New cigarette ash drops

and rolls before taking flight across a paper
ramp corner trying to escape my pen. Wind nests
in an unknown palm of space and I imagine

it may try to work my limbs like a tree, waving
me to distraction, eroding my anchor in this
fragile place of work, whispering what it knows,

that more of me is straining to leave than not.

Temple of the Mud Bank

I stumbled near the creek bank
During a walk on my lunch

Dress shoes sunk to the ankles
Hands stretching, then knuckle deep

Knees then, one and the other
Mud water pooling in cool

Soaking my socks to the skin
Fouling my fresh shoe polish

Cigarette spat from my lips
Landing under my crouched form

Puffing away its incense
Unintentional smudging

I inhale its last tendril
Before it sizzles away

A white message through my nose
Into my lungs and back out

Kneeling before this sudden
Mud-caked alter I have found

Rocks wet with my reflection
The river tuning itself

Before it forks down the way
One to the west and one south

Neither asking my bidding
A river never in need

Of knowing where prayers must go

Dragonfly Questions

Double-twin wings blue flash
a figure-8 dance of death,
a show of amber-armored-bodies
on a summer day's cloudlessness.

All is quiet for the duel,
a beautiful choreographed loop
of the territorial swoop and dodge.

The enternalness of it singing
in the air and obvious.

I wonder if they think
of their ancestors, their giant
pre-historic machinatious kin folk?

Why quarrel with your brother?
For what do you fight? Do you think
on your ancestors? Dream
of your father's fathers still tasting
the long water of their youth?

The oldest dragonflies lived
over 300 million years ago.
Mega Neura: with two-and-a-half-foot
wingspans blotting the sun in loud blurs
and frightening dodges through
the endlessness of canopies, such
beautiful death in combat with everything.

Later, I find a dying dragonfly on a tree leaf,
barely moving, stilled and readying for its
dance with archeology, realizing
one is always the winner.

Blood & Kudzu

I walked the grounds of my conception,
hunting through the crawling green for some
sentimentality, perhaps expecting un-riddled
things to speak from the ground of my past.

I returned, horrified, a confusing smell of Kudzu
and disturbed soil laced in my skin, cocooning any
possibility of reunion. For three days I waited,
reliving the lesson's emptiness, until the last
hints of disappointment floated away.

Nothing remains of where I'm from. No thing.
No struggling root or stem. No whispering sigh.
No half-exposed garbage hinting as to what was.
There is only the clean, guiltless absence of sound,
deep green and slow, moving when you aren't looking.

For Kudzu conspires to murder our memories.
In the deepest summer days its vine and leaf will choke
over a body or a bloodstain—evidence of you—overnight.

This is the best place to kill thoughts of a missing home.

Home

When things finally settle in my neighborhood,
when the kids on four-wheelers and muffler-less

motorcycles quit the day, when the foot traffic
of pill-seeking strangers stumbling the sidewalk

lessens, when I only hear the mumble of conversation
through windows over televisions that glow all night,

I go out to sit on my porch, in the dark, witnessing
it all rotting together into what I can only call home,

the dusky shadows, the smell, its sick energy mixed
and swallowed down into my gut like a disgusting

meal made by a relative you can't and won't refuse.
Part of me wants to run away, the other to stand

my ground, to stay just long enough to eventually
root out the true wealth of this little spot of mine.

Times Square

I hear the concrete expanding
under mid-summer's long yawns,
a seducing vibration itching away
under the heating of my feet,
I-beams relaxing and popping

under years of weight, the crowd

choraling a single voice, lightish
but impenetrable, calling me
to join in my tourist's drawl,
to puzzle in my place with elbows
and dashes of mountain dust

from yesterday's walk in the hills.

I am drenched in neon, the sun
structure-dimmed, slow traffic
circulating a bass resonance,
light-headed from pooled fumes
and perfumes, the exchange

of supper breath from a hundred

countries in a single whiff,
walking the museum cases
of latest fashion and technology,
seduced and in-drawn, self-judgment
my only obstacle from complete

assimilation into the jungle.

Grinder

An August morning heat broils
whatever the sun crawls over.
9 AM and my clothes are soaked
heavy at the job my father got me,
outside the foundry and steel shop
he'll work at for another 20 years,
where my Papaw worked for 30,
where I'll work only a few weeks
until I leave for basic training.

I was handed a ten pound grinder
on the first day, a hardhat, goggles,
a respirator and long leather gloves.
They offered protection, but they
actually encumber you from seeing
and feeling well enough to manage
a safe and efficient job. You must
see clearly, know your fingertips,
to grind and chip the rough edges
from manhole covers all day long.

I boil in all of this grinder's armor,
goggles sweat-filled, glasses fogging,
a sneaky powered gray taste finding
my tongue and throat all evening,
never leaving my nails and ears.
I rub my toes inside the temporary
caps I've tamped onto my surplus
boots and feel the blisters bubbling.
I finally toss the respirator so I can
breath and see and not lose a finger
like my uncle did in the pattern shop.

Five years later, and this same
penetrating heat finds me crouching
in the Mojave Desert, in a trench
half-dug in impossible sand and rock,

my body layered and sealed in a
charcoal lined Nuclear-Biological-
Chemical suit. The 100-degree day
is relentless, windless, everywhere
hovering and baking, the CS Gas
low and lurking on the flat sand.

Unlike the respirator at the grinding
yard, this head-hugging rubberized
alien gasmask can't be removed.
The soppy rubber gloves must stay.
No matter how claustrophobic.
Every inch of me is sealed. This gas
seeks to singe my lungs. Eyes. Skin.

The all clear is finally signaled.
I unseal myself and I'm back
into the world of limitless air
leaving me wondering, and worrying,
who could ever fight, and live,
in this death suit, pouring a half
gallon of sweat out of my mask,
gloves, and rubber boots.

48 hours at camp

The day is summer-stretched
rolled in a damp heat's indifference
visible and coating things in heaviness

urged warmer by a mid-day fire's struggle
insects and lizards growing sleepy
forever lulled by a cicada's mantra

The heat overtakes my writing's shape
dancing with the lean and pressure of script
thinning my ink and baking my writing hand

thoughts finally flattened wide and clear
but running my words into some illegible
cave scribble I will not recognize tomorrow

A bear tore through our campsite

I slept, as you lay awake
watching the quiet lightning,

anticipating the storm.
I woke to charley horses
fist-punched deep into my thigh.

I'd never before smelled fear.
It was undeniable
fear, your inability

to form words that would warn me.
But the scent was obvious,
smacking of paralyzed dread,

a message screaming, *don't move*,
the alchemy of our camp
vibrations overtaken by your

stillness, my thigh still aching,
your wordless state alarming
that something was in the air

more dangerous than the fire,
the now approaching thunder,
our earlier lovemaking.

Your lack of words vacuuming
our tent clean of everything
but the floating scent of fear.

Carpenter Bee and fire coax the evening buzz

from the wood's darkening, their chorused notes
the strongest things in the forest, a perfect *OM* chant,
stilling the ground where so very little rests,
smoke smudging out around the bee as it holds
midflight, more controlled than a humming bird.

It lights, weighing down a weed, then up again
to inspect our fire altar, hovering near my face,
alien and knowing eyes searching through me
without my permission, hummed wings a mantra-tone
with the fire's rhythm, calling a drum circle song
down to the ants turning the ground alive in waves.

The fire collapses and remolds its heat, nothing
is still in the forest edges suddenly, cicadas drone
their planned evensong, high in cloistered branches,
paper-winged but strong, like watchful angels.

The Carpenter Bee finally moves, fading back into
the fog of dusk, remembering where stillness waits.

Water Boil at Camp

The water is finally boiling on the fire.

I'm hovering over its promise, impatient
for the miracle of bubbles at the bottom,

some ghost wisps of steam, like waiting
on the porch for sunrise, knowing it comes,
trusting it since we've been here before.

Stalking it brings no encouragement, but
I'm curious. Something hisses, rumbles noise
from nowhere. How? I don't understand.

Where are the rocks where it tumbles?
The cars splashed? The waterfall? Nothing
pours from the tap, no slapping the roof's tin,
running to gutters, searching out the ground.

It dances and sings from the fire pit,
an exploding world's slow crash, unseen
molecular ruckus, a bubbling mystery I know

I should never want to fully understand.

Crosscuts

Orange-tongued voices crack
dry-throated up from the fire pit.

We're hemmed in by crosscuts
of trees too large to burn,
over-sized wedges, and we are ax-less,
helpless in the face of unworked
dormant promises of warmth,

Four specimens of bark
rest to the side, like salvaged
post-storm body skins,
recently felled and dissected beyond
the camp view over the ridge,

A damp columned cloud fuses the fog,
tree frogs taking over for cicadas,
ash snow hunting familiar ground,

The fire smudges us
with the peeled skin of trees,
hints of epidermis, splintered
vein systems, voiceless,
branchless and leafless,
gnarls and knots of life exposed,

all of it giving way to blackening
in nightfall's slowing promise.

Sleep.

Let me shoo the mosquitos
from your legs and feet,

turn the curious ants in another direction,

try to deflect the beech nuts
falling from the canopy
before they disturb your rest in the mottled sun.

I will occupy the bees with our honeyed stories

and pick the last flower of summer
for your gentle wrist,

tend the fire like it's our last
remaining warmth of the imagined

winter of the mind,
our meal ready when you wake.

Nothing is Straight

In a world of circles and swirls, curves and slopes,
nothing sketched by nature seems truly straight.

No trunk or branch, not the leaf edge or seed skin.
Grasses bend in the swirl of dust, ridges and valleys
grow and crest in waves with the earth's slow tide.

Bodies relax into tidal shapes, filled with hidden
organs, finely curved and puzzled, like once jagged
rocks smoothed with erosion's hug, softened.

The pond's glassiness ripples with the slightest breath.
The sea horizons hint at curvature and even light
bends to the gravity of a million black holes.

But when drawn by humankind's hands, a ridged
straightening follows everywhere. Squared and taut
evidence trails your conquering of the rounded earth:

Crop rows, an obelisk's stony stretch, floors, roofs, rulers,
the line of telephone poles, a bullet's first trajectory.
The unnaturalness of flattened mountaintop ridges,
sidewalks, the leveling and plumbed gravity of men
forcing themselves on the earth's vulnerable curves.

These growls from the forest

come not
from the oldest life there,
for the most ancient beings
are quiet
and refuse to argue
in the emptiness
of words,

jutting their taproots
into the night's cooling
dream nests,

resting in the daylight
heat, full-born,
saturating everything
they touch,

every spot of life
you hide in your valleys,
recoiling in amazement.

The white noise
you mistake
as a peaceful tree line
masks, in quiet lullaby,
the prophesies
you ignore
in your sleepwalk.

Drought

Rain fell, shouted down,
chased from the clouds

by some undreamt of rebel
demons, finally breaking

the back of summer's
stubborn drought, fire

hardened ground crying
relief from under grasses

gone tan and skins gone
brittle, waiting for salvation's

blot of the life-draining sun.

Medicine Bag

Bring me the veins of the first turning leaf
Three scratches from early winter ice cycles
Two identical snowflakes from the pine boughs
A handful of spring rain caught at arm's length
Pinches of bark dust shaved from the Alder
Exhaled Crocus pollen from your lungs
Inhaled scents of summer's warmest decay
Lightening streaks on the overflowing river
The memory of thunder from your youth
A vibration of hoofs on the treeless plains

Mix in the halved scull of your sister deer
Consume the mix under a dying star's light
While going to water and bathing 7 times
Crawl into the earth womb of the sweat lodge
Form a clay ball from your pooling sweat
Fill your bag and clench it close to your heart

Locale Sancti

I swim the vacuum
between your atoms
sing along the dark
mattered strands

between galaxies
beyond imagination
witnessing the base
pattern of all worlds

the mystery scripts
hanging ornamented
about your thoughts
I hum under your feet

within the valleys
of fingerprint ridges
shrinking expanding
destroying creating

my laugh and smiles
wrapping your world
in scales of D flat major
be still and know me

Tsunami

Water monster, darkening the earth
in your mindless roll, black froth eating

and spitting up the sun, quake and fire-borne,
spare my family that run to the hills,

my quiet and simple home, my life,
my breath, all I am and care to be and think,

spare this town, spare us the memory
of your wake's thousand absorbed faces,

their stuttered prayers mid-thought
in scurried horror, your anger splintering

and drowning the rising sun and all it falls
upon, lacking the face of an understood god.

Sing the Dead

I would sing the dead from the ground.
Stir them up clear from their dust,
coaxed high through the long six feet.
Who living recollects the songs of the dead?
How deeply the voice must echo,
how tightly to hug with a right vibration,
how close to their sleeping ears?

What is this obsession, this odd rehearsal,
not of death, but the full leading up to it?

In my dream my hands are gloved in mud,
boots sucked slurping down in the deep,
arms wrestling a shovel, slapping dark water
up out of the hole, a muddy cascade back
in my face, over and over, getting nowhere.
I've dug too deep. No voice yells the warning down.
I just feel it, as suddenly as the sun giving way to shadow.
What song lingers in the heavy absence of sun,
this hint of serenade lingering in the shadows?

In my dream I flee with smells of recent rain
and the dead's dust pressing damp the cloak
on my back and shoulders, weighting me down,
waiting down in the somewhere for me.

Have I retrieved that for which I searched,
between the mounds of fresh and dangerous earth?
So diligently between the towers of lightless stone?
So absent-heartedly between the memories
I've made up to fill in the gaps?

I think back at the many bodies I've seen.
Standing in polite lines, staring down on faces.
I can't see them without wondering—but don't we all
wonder how we'll look—laying there silk framed—
and wonder still on what we'll look like before

the mortician commences—as to what event
brings us merging arm-in-arm with such rest—
whether anyone might notice hints in our faces
as to what done us finally in—the dead talk,
and pray, and sing and commune. And having forever,
their whispered words nearly imperceptible,
take the rest of our lives to sing out the one word: live.

Meaning

There are days when everything means everything,

polarized against others when all is the frightening
pit of meaninglessness. Who is immune to the inner
script of an empty end or, on better days, a hero's
mysterious story in a world that screams both
symbolism and blankness as the bitterest of kin.

We must lean in, and we do, and we fail and falter,

sometimes emerging slightly scathed and hardened
against our silly demons, realizing how sky quakes,
earth sounds and flock deaths, fish kills, bee plagues
and rivers of snakes and winter tornados are neither
curses nor blessings, but are just simple questions.

This poem betrays me and I leave you in bed

I leave you in bed, an unwritten poem betraying me,
too early Saturday morning, alarm lying its urgency
of the day. I'm awake whether I want it or not.
I leave you wrapped under the down quilt upstairs,
oak floor cold and shocking my senses as I set up
to write, to quietly search the words that woke me.

My stuttered tap-tapping is distracting, oddly similar
to the slurp-tinks of the coffeemaker I started up there.
I hope the sounds and dark scents won't disturb you.
I have a feeling I can't write this with you awake.
You have to be up there, don't you? Oblivious.
Eyes clamped in the bliss of stress-less sleep.

I run to poetry when you're gone, these weeks between
weekends, when we're not attached at the hip and always
on our first date, again and again. But having to write
this down, right now, betrays me, yanks me sleepless
from the soft angled nest of your hip I fell asleep upon.
Steals our little space of time, the air we might share.

Incense of the downstairs sitting room: a teaspoon
of red wine in the bottle, cork fragrance, cigarette ash
in a cup, red stained cup lip, your scent on my tapping
fingers mixed with the grounds I scooped by hand,
hint of perfume at neck level on the chair, a heavy rain
out in the dark you would want to know was falling.

The question rises

without permission, like the sun or moon.
You must struggle with this question,
with where it leads, with what it asks of you.

A tree once stood here, did it not?
I'm sure of it, you think. *I'm sure.*
Look around, find your bearings,
remember your time here before.
Stare at the sawdust under your feet,
fresh with the faintness of gasoline
soaked into what remains of this
newly lit place warmed by the sun
for the first time in 88 years.
Count the rings in that discarded
cross-section of heart and mind.

Yes, a tree was here once, was it not?
I'm sure of it, you think. *I'm sure.*

When you were here before, did you
recognize it quietly watching,
listening to your every thought?
Did you thank its straight strength,
acknowledge its mid-day shelter?
Did you promise to honor it again,
with the protection of your company?

A tree once lived here you can be sure.
And that tree was run down and killed here,
in the truth-seeking light of day, while we
toiled indoors, choked from its view,
ignoring the machine's threats, insulated
from our guilt, the familiar exhaust,
from the sudden quiet in the field.

I'm sure of it.

When Birds Fell

This is the year birds fell from the sky,
with winter full on, the opposite of snow
flung from the sky in a dark, flapping rain,

frozen mid-flight amid normal conversation,
to the muted and unforgiving ground, throats
and wings and nests and next meals silenced:

On roofs, heads, back yards, streets, sidewalks,
car hoods, driveways, swimming pools, fields,
porches, play grounds, trees and rivers banks.

We will be finding them well into next year
until the mystery reawakens, searching again for
winged sacrifice and another means of waking us.

Find me the strong web

to string my soul along,
memory flashes like beads
of morning fog dotting
a temporary framework,
mysteries sealed in reflecting
spheres so delicate a merest
consideration threatens this
delicate house of a thousand
vibrating mirrors, steadily
shrinking, morning sun drying
them away to forgetfulness.

Find me the stubborn bark
to carve my soul's song within,
scratched dark alien runes
tossed too long ago to remember
clearly, but hummed in a new
tune down some yawning roots
stretching into the creek banks.

Find me an ancient spring to set
these words upon, broken free
by earth's quake, dust disturbed
and loosed off the forgotten glass
of the mind, false foundations
split and injured, but quieted
in the meditation of surprise.

Answer to an elegy

For Jesse Graves

They disappear, don't they? These reminders
we want to hold so tightly, even in the rusting
impossibility of it all. But the important things
are nearly un-trackable, once they've made up
their minds and set out on lives we rarely consider.

The mind's trinkets leach out on travels in our sleep,
less sharp with each accidental glance, like undusted
tools neglected under the harshness of summer rain,
decay-born, slipping back into that sleep by nightfall,

without so much as a peep of protest, no regret,
no farewell songs of pain, a ghost's strolling finale
beyond sight, through the screen door, off the porch
and down the road to another haunt without us.

Part II

Friday Day

Please don't ask me to divine the day.
The tea sachet spins counter-clockwise on Friday the 13th.
A column of ember morphs to long drips
Slows and vanishes so obviously like lives.
There will be no tea leaves left in the cup to wonder on.
Who troubles themselves for tea in cemeteries any longer?
Not even the grave-witchers stay past twilight.

> friday night
> who can divine the bloodied night,
> the mantra, *Oh mon Dieu*, quieted
> on the thousand cell phone-lit lips
> of stun-stepped Parisians, slacked
> faces pre-dawn brightened, eyes un-blinking,
> drifting up in unison from the old alleys
> of stone-cobble, a shaky-handed prayer
> overpowering the scent of smoke and fear.

Crow Sun

A single crow calls its intention over the day's snow shroud.
Sky and ground share a color, competing in their bluing white.
Only trees, a barn, power lines, a hill's dimming silhouette,
defy the sky's hunger and they, too, are losing the struggle.
The crow knows its present place, the high thrust limb,
its perch like a wounding crack working into the sky's hunger.

The crow calls its intention through the day's snow shroud,
louder than the windless snow, the darkest thing visible,
shaking off the snowflakes not melting from its black warmth.

I will serve as the sun today, it calls. *I will serve, I will serve.*

Solstice & Eclipse

The night's longest thought bears down on us.
The myth-sayers mumble signs and promises
and curses around the evening fires as winter
finally agrees to breathe. The ground remains
ice-solid, snow-worn, long-ready for nightfall.

A full moon will bless the between, enlivened,
high and slow, calling. In this longest dark,
an eclipse will give chase and softly devour
the moon, but never again like this. Never,
at least, that any of us will see in our lives.

I know I can't wait that long.

The synchronicity cannot be ignored.
Tonight I must wake to the sky blood,
walk to the cold, under the night sun,
view the promise, bleeding and awesome.

Will I take this blanketing past the dawn
of the year's shortest day, the sun tired,
low and fast in a sky caring not
what magic transpired while it slumbered?

Death of Porches

Front porches are a dying thing.
Rockers and swings, hanging baskets,
your late evening sip of bourbon
in the forgiving death of the day's heat,
the neighbor visiting, traffic's creep,
a dog's bark, all of it myth-bound.

Our new architecture neglects the idea.
Opts for decks out back, inconsequential
foyers where no one lingers any longer
than to dust off shoes or hang an umbrella.

The saved space makes room for garages
consuming a third of a house's façade,
sacrifices closet space for empty halls,
asphalt double driveways over the little
bit of space for a garden you may have had.
Plastic potted plants in conditioned air.

This is fear. Fear of what might be seen
if we kept our porches and sat there, rocking,
breathing, looking neighbors in the eye,
accidently catching our own reflections.

All this writing on things,

these long bouts
with duplicating
misunderstood

moments, is really
just wanting to travel
somewhere

I've never heard
of, to birth some
immortal oddity

on the side
of the mountain,
abandon it

only partially
hidden, so
when you happen

upon this stumbling
and naked creature
on the trail,

you will look around
to make sure
no one is watching

while secreting
it away in your coat
to make it yours.

By the time you realize you're a ghost

it's too late. There is no re-memory, no
re-winding of the un-done. But at least

you can't remember what you never fixed
before. And what you've forgotten might

have been important can't frustrate or hurt
you much. You can grow accustomed

to that nagging tug, like flashes of dread
washing over you when you're two hours

into a trip and begin worrying if you've
turned off the iron or the hair straightener,

or when you feel that strange vibrating
hum and distant light at night and force

yourself to go down to the kitchen to check
if you've left the refrigerator door open.

The Great Snow

Once the snow commenced I knew
what the voices had meant.
                            The sound of wings in my sleep
roused me, beat an off-rhythm warning on the drum
of my unbelieving heart.

> *It will begin snowing soon,*
> *It will begin snowing soon.*

Outside, through my cigarette smoke,
I could smell and taste it.
                    Snow in the dark,
low and cradled through hollows in the East,
        high above and laced into swirls
                        snaking nearer while the rest of my world
                                                slept.

Who will listen to me, frightening snow angels?

It matters not who will listen, they mouthed,

> *Only that you speak.*

They created winter

The gods created winter so
that poetry might first exist,

beginning all things with the icy rock,
hoisting the rain in hardened form,

shaping the land with iced wedges
the size of the first thousand hands.

That Eden was the only world of verse,
roamed by the natural poets, one freshly

missing a rib, the other shunning fear,
their paradise land-locked by glassy walls

of ice lifting just too far away the place
they longed to dwell, if only in words.

Snow Blind

I stand reading from a new book of poetry,
late morning sun heating my back, my head

shadowing the page, that peripheral blinding
glow of mostly white space on the next page

unless I shift the book or tilt my head, protecting
myself from the lost sight I'd suffer looking

directly into the dangerously empty white.

We do this sometimes—intentionalize
our shadows over things we know will hurt,

softening the view, staring sideways, knowing
that what *could* happen is safer than glancing

too close to the promise of the next page.

**Additional thoughts on the weight
and possible location of the soul:**

Something like a hug, columned up
from forests we always tiptoe through,
color-flavored with equal parts guilt
and bliss that drift from artesian sources
of love and regret, smoke-battled
on the limbs and soft-dented,
shadowing the odd life walk,
only a tendril of connection holding on,
nearly forgotten, but clung to like
buried albums wrapped in roots,

or, is the soul a lost blind poem,
ever-circulating its dance in your limbs,
sensing your hunt for it with new words,
but going to ground when your imagination
draws closer, resting under root-large arteries,
brushing past the heart, loitering safely,
holding its breath, burrowing into bone
to your long-cavish marrow, that
tastiest morsel in the feast of evasion.

Spirit Coil

The spirit moves
  skins and lays me up

to rest and dry
  cooling near death

like the spent rattler
  after a daylong service

The tongue silenced
  but coiled like a spring

my mouth slacked into
  a hungry trap in the air

snapping at the dreams
  tamborined into tears

readying for alien tides
  of words vibrating awake

from hibernating in fear
  of darkening prophecy

Star Blind

Sometimes I stare down a star,
the brightest one I can find, one
most demanding my attention,
calling up with the inner voice

only deep and empty space will
understand, the traffic, lights,
my own limbs even, fading
into the silence of periphery.

I am quieted for a moment,
as if the only being gazing up
to this light, imagining its stare
of personality, knowingness,

mirroring a similar wonder,
smiles in remembrance
of speaking out the answers to my
endless questions a billion years ago.

Stretch

A silent cold proclaims the thing,
wordless, self-assured, shivering
into its mantle of red to orange,
to pink, swirled blue to space black,

bleeding streaks on eastern ridges,
mountain rolling mute and smooth,
foreground split by the bare tree's
song of morning wind and memory.

Meet autumn's morning ferocity
sliding the ridge, blinding the brave
who care to notice a hint of heat
and glancing up to meet the light,

then down again, as shadows thin,
for what is spared the long lit stretch,
asphalt bumps, long-wormed along,
gravel specks pealed long as hills,

grass and fingers tall as trees, or
souls drawn off across the lot
bent angled up the brick facade
or vanished in the tree-lined field.

Run

Even in our blind sprint from death
we fly nearer, ears clamped against

the quickened floor creaks creeping
behind us, searching something out

to distract ourselves enough to forget
what must wait in the next mysterious

room we've avoided since moving
into this old house.

        But we relent,

giving in, finally, feeling it in the murk,
herding us, alarmingly closer, a scent

matching ours, steadying a hot breath
when it hears us sliding open the bolt,

to find it still standing there waiting,
scratching notes on the peeling walls.

Dancing with the Red Haired Lady

After Sylvia Plath's "Lady Lazarus"

The promise of resurrection is like a calling card
of faith in effort—this ink, nodded over, with confused
shakes of the head as you struggle to mean something
after no longer owning any of the air's property.

Make some plan for how the tenants following on might
happen across your boxed up, crumpled, and dehydrated
spirit. Perhaps take pity and put it up in a window box
with a few cups of water from the tap to see what happens.

Grow me back when you find me. Lend a moment
of your life back into these final ones I enjoyed
and I will reward you with a possession of my fate,
a walk in the inner sanctums and staircases winding

some places that never knew light—*Lady Lazarus* and I—
dancing in the dark, now lit by your fragile curiosities.

May you know lightning

in the heart of a snowstorm,
with terror and soothing
all at once, a coppery taste
faint on your tongue's muted

surprise, as the thunder wraps
your core in the secret language,
dropping down into vibrations
you may never want to feel,
but the heart has always known.

May it flash open something
within you, cracking fully wide
the cage of your soul's silence,
birthing your heart-rooted wings,
as blinding as the storm you fear.

Someone said, "Let there be light...

and unanswered pleas for clarity
accusation and blame on the weak
happenings which allude the witness
miracles missed in the light of day
life-ending mysteries in the nights
so-called good killings and bad killings
separated families thrown to the winds
mountains of money made and lost
greed without the possibility of end
unshakable faith born of desperation
unbelievable and mistaken answers
blankets and pillows of loneliness
confused tongues aimed into silent skies
rivers of blood and stacked dead things
stuttered prophesy and the terror of vision
the constancy of earthquakes
minds ever-churning *sturm und drang*
lightning strikes on the sinless
confirmed rumors of war
hell-scaring truths repeated
the deaf and the deafening envied
mutations of muted fields
demons threatening from under beds
closets crowded with horrible sounds
hordes of hungry forest things
myths and their famous myth-makers
doom makers and drama fakers
heroes sought and mocked
and faith among the insane."

Cold Cipher

Wind whispers the only word
it remembers over the glass.

Outside is an expanding math
problem of flurries and fog

and ice sparkle, revealing
the wind's hiding places,

white tornadoes dancing
across an empty parking lot,

the hills fading and moaning
back into sleep, the white crows

gathering up one another
to cipher their discoveries.

In winter, when the craziness stirs,

I awake already in the snow-sleep,
trudging against the wind and dark,
ice-stumbled and arguing poetry
against the air's relentless bite
into the yawns of my clothes.
These thoughts on verse are colder
than the wind, stubborn and stuck
and clear-glass. A numbing slice
over the tips of my ears reminds me
I've forgotten a hat in my sudden rush
to get outside and track down what might
have broken the snow before sundown.
Out there in the quiet view, with only
the sound of freezing blood and ideas
and careful steps, is where I may
find the phrase I lost upon waking.

The drifts are shadowed orange,
like painted dunes from a high view.
I stop to rest. A leaf scratches along
the snow's pack like the *tap, tap, tink*
of an invisible ice pick, tumbled in
wandering, dangerous in its blindness.
Snow changes its mind and charges
a swirled dodge sneaking from behind,
loitering in the branches, hugging
the corners of empty buildings
with lights left on. The ground cracks
like colorless stained glass, my reflection
down there underfoot somewhere.
I retrace my way, my steps nearly
covered from earlier, in daylight,
when I followed another's trail,
wondering why they were going
in the same direction as me.
A crow calls. Odd in the dark, but safe.
Hush, there. They will know you're here.

Hush, keep watch over where I go
in search of that dream I've lost.

Nesting

There are spots I search
out on your body,
the nest in your shoulder,
the saddle of your hip,

the small sweep
of your back, your wrists,
where, when I rest
my head, my world exhales

and finally falls away
at the end of the day,
when my mind is inspired
and clarified, splendid

in a prolonged instance
of finest working order.
But when I shift
it fades a bit, so I hold on,

stilling myself,
reaching back in
for the language
I only hear
when half-curled

into your perfection.

Snails are Probably Deists

A dense meandering of trail glistening
in the evening's late sun along the concrete
sidewalk catches my eye. A secret event,
evidence visible at a certain perfect angle.

What happened seems clear to me.
A snail wanders off the safer grass here,
along the bleached concrete, circling then
into fits of wild figure eights, then straight

and clean for a while with new purpose,
close to the edge but turning, drifting again,
the silvery slime echoing a day of frustration
stretched along ten feet, before the snail,
finally dried beyond movement, dies, head
straining up, inches from the sweet grass.

Had I been there to watch, it wouldn't
have been aware I was witness to its long
struggle, my curious company too immense
for snail language to comprehend. After all,
snails don't know what they don't know.
But I want it to know that I'm sad,
standing here now, thinking of its ordeal.

It's a sorry, weak analogy, isn't it?

You struggled, small creature, yes. Where you
were going was mostly unknown, but you went.
Your journey was near impossible, but gorgeous.
I was probably somewhere nearby and might
have helped, but your voice can be so small.
I see your journey now, your every step.
Though alone, you were not fully abandoned.

72-degree mid-February day

a lone honey bee wanders the air
yawning some stiff memory of flight
abruptly awake and called out of safety
to duty by a whisper understood only
as an ancient vibration of color and taste
methodical over mostly absent green
landscape bloomless but for plastic flowers
marking other still hibernating things

The crocuses sound confused
with their little preemptive voices
of purple and yellow and white
too early Easter eggs perhaps
winking up to light's surprise
the clouds now darkening with coolness
but laced of Saffron and offering
only the scent of a final mission

I swear I can smell things
under the ground sometimes
heavy dirt hints at where the Irises
and Spearmint are spreading
where the Crocuses are strolling
are these as dormant as we suspect
or do they keep vigil with the most
diligent bees who dare to roam in winter?

Standing Chimneys

I'm fascinated with lone standing chimneys.
I've wondered what it takes to survive
a fire, or be intentionally preserved, mantle
stripped, exposed and vertical in vague
stubborn purpose for our random questions.

I have an intense dislike of half-opened gates
leading to nothing, bookended by strips
of fencing - house, foundation, chimney gone.
This feels like a misplaced invitation
for re-beginning, without a single nail,
or splinter, or bit of the concrete sidewalk,
or shade tree left with which to start over.

It's frightening. That a half-hearted inviting
gate would be all we have, with little else
than oblivion actually lurking at our rusting
entrances, that not a charred chimney brick
or chip of bleached mortar might remain of us
past the ghostly welcome, un-hearthed.

**If we looked forward,
deep enough and without**

much fear, we might catch
the echo of our mistakes,

our recent stumblings,
our past delusions armored

against sense. The repetitive
hum like last breaths,

the hills no longer hills,
a flattened drone of sand

and clay, the hollows drilled
and scooped empty,

the anticipated green now
our vacant glass of tired air,

nothing familiar, like captured
signals from a distant

world once bright, but
long removed of life sounds.

And this is magic:

lightning and thunder, all at once ceasing
the terrible downpour, sun and moon,
competing in the sky sea, water voices

interpreting cave paintings, learning a new
language of endless skin, cicadas and frogs
louder than the car engines and laughter,

the hydration of reading, the miracle
of death in the fall and the rumored
promise of green to come, the sounds

of curling shadow bones, the scent
of the storm flipping the color of leaves,
and breathing through your fingertips,

a suddenness of spider webs on your neck,
an ancient communication of fingerprints,
the mind's perfect blindness in sleep,

angst at the atomic level you cannot explain,
stepping out of the darkness of hesitancy,
rubbernecking along our human wreckage,

a footstep's space as an entire universe,
eating every meal as if it's your last,
quilt squares as prayer flags in the sun,

catching the whisper of your inner
alien language, leaving cairns behind,
and misplacing fear but not minding.

Honey in the Jar

I now hide this memory of you
in a jar of soon-forgotten honey,

sacrificed and lifted to a high shelf,
welcoming the dust and darkness,

your slowing thought a speck of comb
sealed and flash-frozen in a thickness

not nearly as sweet as one hint of you
caught in the ambering of my mind.

The Weighing

I: The Experiment and Resulting Inquiries

> A doctor experimented with measuring the mass
> of the soul as it left the body of several patients.
> The results varied, an average mass of 21 grams.
> Believed by some, mocked and discredited by others,
> he left us a curious legacy of questions as to what
> was happening as his subjects died on his industrial
> scale. More so, why something as mysteriously
> important, so spiritually hefty as a human's soul,
> varies from test to test and ultimately weighs so little.

What, by comparison, falls within
a range of less or more than 21 grams?

> *A buckeye. A flashdrive. A Gideon's Bible.*

What items do we touch each day, the masses
of which mirror the mass our own evasive souls?

> *A house key. A bottle of painkillers. A broken condom.*
> *The cumulative leaves on the porch after a storm.*

Might our souls have passed along the hand,
cupped for an instant accidentally in our palms?

> *Half pack of smokes. All your credit cards. An ink pen.*
> *A dried Cicada skin. Lint in your pocket. Box of razors.*

And, more importantly, perhaps, what influences
vary the mass of one soul against another?

> *A cumulative measure of too much or too less:*
> *Guilt. Joy. Grief. Envy. Bliss. Confusion. Pain.*
> *Shame. Laughter. Sin. Betrayal. Fear. Faith.*
> *Empathy. Apathy. Loneliness. Ecstasy. Dread.*
> *Love. Love. Love. Lovers. Love. Love. Love.*

II: Other Mass-influencing Considerations

> Did this eccentric physician appropriately take
> into account other mass influencing variables?
> What is the mass of one's last earthly breath?
> Does an amount of a last inhalation remain
>
> in the lungs? Did he consider the possibility
> that, at the instance of death, a gnat, too small
> to be noticed by the doctor as it landed near
> the lips before commencing, was startled away
>
> as the patient slowly exhaled, the weight of this
> last portion of breath and gnat combining enough
> to cause some fraction of a fraction's difference?
> Did the patient's eyes fill with tears of laughter
>
> and anticipation, or fear and dread, rivering down
> and finally drawing off the cheek? Does one's
> cumulative memories and dreams, millions
> of these, cause a sudden measurable vacuum?

III: Comparability Summary

But when we consider that all the mass within
the known Universe is an expanding explosion
originating from a point no larger than a pin head,
it is possible to believe that a few grams of mass
might very well house our entire spiritual story:

> *Every bruised knee. Prayer launched into the dark.*
> *Clasped hand. Donated organ. Scream in orgasm.*
> *Whisper of doubt. Fingertip along familiar skin.*
> *Color change of aura. Falling in and out of love.*
> *Every fleeting instant we understood, and forgot.*

White Crow (Catcher of the Last Snow Flake)

The trees paint the mountainsides again, fresh and glad,
pollinating the senses, dancing with the faintness of a field's
first mowing. A crow eyes down, whispering her mantra,
Be Watchful, Be Watchful. Yes, Mother. I am watchful.

Abandoning her prayer branch, she climbs the morning wind
in silence. Winter has yet to give in, she knows. She heeds
its rumored plans for a final argument of protesting chill,
some gasp of frustration understood only by her kind.

Gorging on late winter carrion for weeks, she ended
her binge this morning. Feeding now only on sunlight
and wind, her dark-fast commences as she waits
for the hint of change across her feathers and eyes.

She circles, watching, not down on the world, but up,
listening for the sunlight to cool, riding high enough
to aim her head, tuck her wings to dive when the time
comes, as her mother taught. *Daughter, Daughter.*
You must fly with no rest until your work is finished.

A whisper forms, laced in clouds that fight the sun,
blue ages to gray, air flavors with threats of snow.
Lightening streaks the storm by night. Tossed about,
dodging hail in swirls of black, she holds fast,
staring where none perceive importance, flying, flying,
with no end, the sun blotted out, her body laden in crystal.
Time dissolves. The storm must pass before she rests.

The sun lives and the storm dies. Ice lightens to flake,
but her burden remains, lines of legend in her
mother's voice heavier than her ice crusted wings.
She is spent, aloft only with the wind's agreement.

At last, a final snowflake forms and descends.
She spots its high lilt, aims stiff wings fit only
for diving, for catching it, a last meal, her tongue

moistened enough only for last happy cries. She closes
her eyes, falling head-first, her newly white body
lost to the ground snow, her gullet's precious seed safe.

Square Inch of Earth

What awaits in the square inch of ground
at my toe? My heel? What world hunches,
heads down, as I step, praying its own
special, *Save us, O Lord,* from such a great
pressing threatening from above, the sudden
dark looming, the wars and rumors of war.

Be thou with us in our hours of confusion,
in our breathless needs to need, turn the sun
back to our eyes, chase this giant burden
from our lives and right us again in mercy.

Again in mercy. Again and again. Amen.

What prays up from the square inch of earth?
And do we ever listen and hear the voices?
The grasses and soils, the words of green,
the black stone, the trudge of microbial feet,
the snails long song sung along leaf veins,
the ant's hard dragging of bark or stem.

What hesitates to exhale down in the deepest
and smallest squares of dirt? It all has much
to say, I imagine, the terrain, the scents
of smallness, the less inclined by gravity,
yet heaven bound. Ever wingless in prayer.

Not quite ingratiated. Again, in mercy. *Amen.*

Larry D. Thacker is a Kentuckian poet, writer, and artist now hailing from Johnson City, Tennessee with his wife, Karin, and their cat, Abraham Lincoln. A five year veteran of the US army and having served fifteen years in the realm of student services in higher education, he finally paid heed to the voices of adventurous reason and will soon complete his poetry and fiction MFA at West Virginia Wesleyan College. He earned his bachelor of history, master of education in counseling, and education specialist degree from Lincoln Memorial University, home of the Mountain Heritage Literary Festival. *Besides Drifting in Awe*, he is the author of *Mountain Mysteries: The Mystic Traditions of Appalachia* (2007), and the chapbooks *Voice Hunting* (2011) and *Memory Train* (2015). His poems have appeared in over a hundred journals and magazines. Keep up with what's happening at www.larrydthacker. com and on Instagram at: thackalachia

www.ingramcontent.com/pod-product-compliance
Lightning Source LLC
Chambersburg PA
CBHW021154090426
42740CB00008B/1089